JUN - 9 2017

Understanding Coding like a

PROGRAMMER

Patricia Harris

PowerKiDS
press.

New York

Published in 2017 by The Rosen Publishing Group, Inc.
29 East 21st Street, New York, NY 10010

First Edition

Editor: Caitie McAneney
Book Design: Michael J. Flynn

Photo Credits: Cover (boy using computer) Samuel Ashfield/Science Photo Library/Getty Images; cover, pp. 1, 3–24 (coding background) Lukas Rs/Shutterstock.com; p. 5 (bottom) ESB Essentials/Shutterstock.com; p. 5 (top left) Blend Images/Shutterstock.com; p. 5 (top right) Kaspars Grinvalds/Shutterstock.com; p. 7 VGstockstudio/Shutterstock.com; p. 8 India Picture/Shutterstock.com; p. 9 Dan Bannister/Getty Images; p. 11 dotshock/Shutterstock.com; p. 13 (top) Photobank gallery/Shutterstock.com; p. 13 (bottom) Andrey_Popov/Shutterstock.com; p. 15 Jacek Chabraszewski/Shutterstock.com; p. 16 Olimpik/Shutterstock.com; p. 17 Caiaimage/Robert Daly/OJO+/Getty Images; p. 21 Bruce Laurance/The Image Bank/Getty Images; p. 22 photastic/Shutterstock.com.

Cataloging-in-Publication Data

Names: Harris, Patricia.
Title: Understanding coding like a programmer / Patricia Harris.
Description: New York : PowerKids Press, 2017. | Series: Spotlight on kids can code | Includes index.
Identifiers: ISBN 9781499427950 (pbk.) | ISBN 9781499428254 (library bound) | ISBN 9781499428834 (6 pack)
Subjects: LCSH: Computer programming–Juvenile literature.
Classification: LCC QA76.73.P98 H35 2017 | DDC 005.1–dc23

Manufactured in the United States of America

CPSIA Compliance Information: Batch #BW17PK: For Further Information contact Rosen Publishing, New York, New York at 1-800-237-9932

Contents

A Problem and a Solution

Many people are afraid of learning about coding. They believe that they could never understand coding or think like a programmer thinks. However, computer programmers don't have superpowers. Instead, they use an organized way of thinking called computational thinking.

Computational thinking involves solving problems. It also involves using thinking skills to recognize what you know and don't know. Programmers break big problems into smaller parts. They organize their solution so it can be put in place. Then they test the solution to make sure it actually solves the problem.

Computational thinking isn't just for computer programmers. It's used by anyone who wants to solve problems effectively—whether or not a computer is involved.

Computer programmers think similarly to other professionals such as doctors and architects. They try to figure out the problem that needs to be fixed and then **implement** the solution.

What's the Big Problem?

The first step in thinking like a programmer is **defining** the big problem. You must know what problem needs to be solved. This may seem **obvious**, but sometimes people try to code before they really know what they want the program to do.

Maybe you have a program that keeps track of your schedule. However, it shows all the entries in black. You want your soccer practice times to stand out. So, you add the ability to show the color green to your program. However, the program either makes every entry green or you have to add the color green for soccer times whenever you go into the program. You may realize that the big problem wasn't adding a color. The big problem was making the program recognize an entry for soccer and make that entry green.

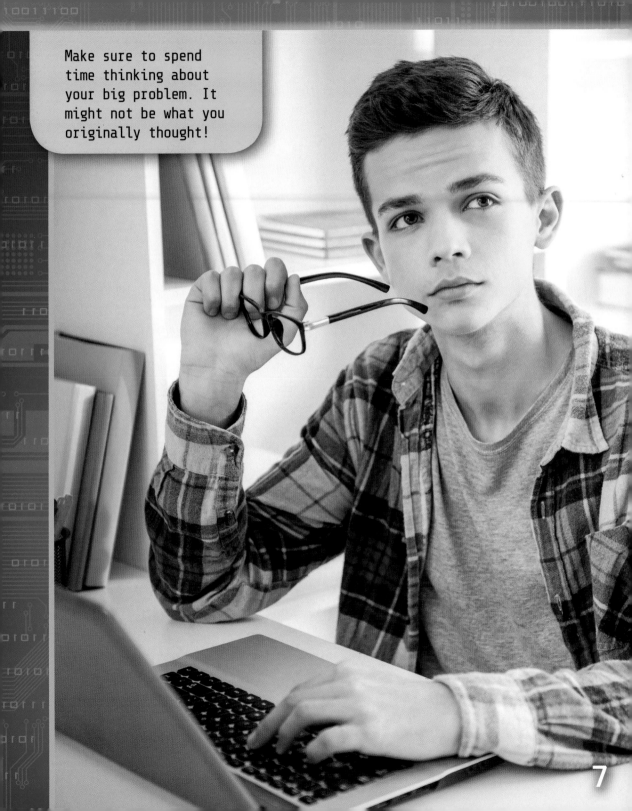

Make sure to spend time thinking about your big problem. It might not be what you originally thought!

What Do You Know?

Programmers also have to think about what they know and what they don't know. You probably think this way without being aware of it. Imagine you need to buy a birthday present for a friend. With little effort, you consider what you know about your friend and what you don't know. You know your friend likes board games because you often play games at their house. You don't know if your friend has the newest release of their favorite game.

Programmers think this way when they begin to write a new program or change one that was already written. For example, they might know what work needs to be done, but they might not know the skills of the people who will be using the program.

You might think like a programmer when you're making snacks for class. You know that your class really enjoys cupcakes and chocolate, but you may not know if anyone has a food allergy.

9

Smaller Parts

Another thinking activity for programmers is splitting big problems into smaller parts. You probably use this way of thinking in school. It's a good **strategy** for completing difficult math problems.

Programmers who work for a company often work as part of a team. Each member of the team may have programming skills that other members don't have. The team may break a big problem into smaller parts and then each member may write one or more of the smaller parts. When the separate parts are done, a programmer can **incorporate** all the separate parts to make a whole program.

It's important that the team communicates about their parts and that each team member only does their part of the work. Then the program parts can work together as a whole program.

Software companies often have teams of programmers work together on big projects.

Let's Reuse Parts!

You don't have to buy new shoes every morning. It would take a lot longer to get ready for school if you did! Instead, you reuse your shoes over and over, and it just takes a minute to put them on.

Programmers also have to think about reusable parts when they're writing programs. First, they need a way to identify reusable parts. The reusable part may be a **variable** or a **routine** that completes a task, often called a **module**. Programmers need to **define** variables in their program so they can call on them again. They also need to think about steps that can be put into a module to use again. They may even need to write the module outside of the main program and save it in a special library.

Breaking the Code

Modules are sections of finished code that can be plugged into larger programs. This allows coders to save time by using code that's already been written. You might think of modules like the legs of a table. Each leg is exactly the same and each is connected to the tabletop to make a finished table. The same table leg can be used to make many tables. Coded modules can be attached to many different programs.

Reusing modules helps programmers write their programs faster.

Reusing Ways of Thinking

Just as programmers reuse modules, they can also reuse their ideas to solve new computer problems in programming. When you learned to solve division problems in math, you may have used your **prior** knowledge of solving multiplication problems. Similarly, programmers often reuse methods learned from solving old problems when solving new ones.

Perhaps a programmer has already written a program to allow users to add the state name to an address using a list of state names that drop down on the screen. The programmer can then reuse that knowledge to create similar drop-down lists with different information. The list structure will be the same, but the information in the list will be different. Reusing old methods for new problems means the programmer can be more **efficient**.

Choose a State ⌄

Alaska
Alabama
Arkansas
Arizona
California
Colorado
Connecticut
Delaware
Florida
Georgia
Hawaii
Iowa
Idaho
▼

Think of your math homework. How do you solve new problems with prior knowledge?

15

Reusing in Real Life

How can you reuse your ideas for new problems in real life? These new problems can be everyday issues, such as your sister or brother hogging your favorite game.

You can reuse your ideas from when you faced this problem, or one like it, in the past. Think about what you did before that solved a problem or made the problem worse. Maybe you complained to your mom about your brother using your game, but you just got in trouble for not sharing. That didn't help. Maybe giving your brother or sister a set time to play your game was enough to make them happy. That *did* help. You can apply that knowledge to solve the current problem. That may help end a fight between you and your sibling in record time!

Reusing program parts and knowledge helps you become more efficient at a certain task or challenge.

Data Structures

Programmers must think about the data structures they need. Data structures are ways of organizing data so that a computer can use it. The better the data structure, the faster the computer can **access** data and complete a job.

Think of data structures as ways to organize items so they can be found easily. You could just pile all your clothes in a big heap on the floor. However, that's not a smart way to organize your clothes. The heap would have clean clothes and used clothes piled together. It would take a while to find your favorite shirt or matching socks! Similarly, if programmers don't organize their data, the computer will have to take more time to find the information it needs.

Breaking the Code

An array is a list of variables under one variable name. For example, an array of your favorite foods might look like this: myfruits = (oranges, pears, apples, grapes). If you want to print the first item in the array, you would use the statement "print myfruits[0]." The first item in a list if called the zero item. If you print "myfruits[1]" you get the word "pears" on the screen. If you print "myfruits" you will see the whole list on the screen.

Sometimes data is stored in an **array** or list. Sometimes it's stored in a tree format. These are two common data structures, but there are many others.

ARRAY

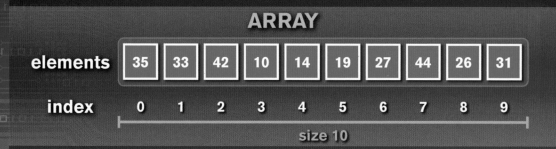

elements	35	33	42	10	14	19	27	44	26	31
index	0	1	2	3	4	5	6	7	8	9

size 10

TREE

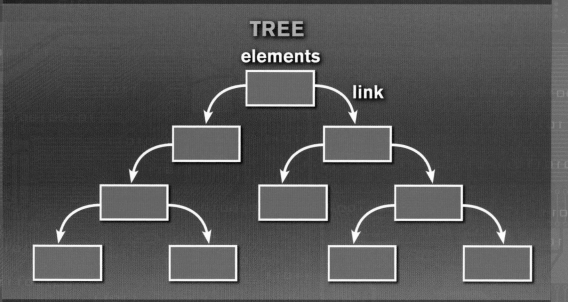

elements

link

Testing a Program

When they finish a program, programmers must ask the question: is this work really correct? To find out, they must test the program parts and the whole program.

When you check your work in math or edit a paper, you're using this way of thinking. Imagine you're writing an important paper. When you finish, you need to check spelling, grammar, and punctuation. You also have to make sure your paragraphs are organized. Then you need to reread your paper to make sure the whole paper makes sense. In the same way, programmers test the parts of their programs and then test the whole program to be sure the parts work together. If even one part is incorrect, it could ruin the whole program.

Breaking the Code

Computer programmers use debugging tools when testing code. The tools are usually a part of the programming environment. These environments are called integrated development environments (IDE). An IDE shows places in the code that have syntax errors, or errors in the ways the words are put together. This happens before you run your code.

Testing a computer program is a lot like editing a paper. The time you spend fixing your mistakes is just as important as the time it took to write the paper the first time.

Practicing like a Programmer

How can you practice thinking like a programmer if you don't know how to code? One example is a math game. You will need paper, a pencil, and two dice. Write down the number 100 at the top of the paper. Roll the dice to get two numbers. Your goal is to get from 100 to 0 as quickly as possible. Decide which operation—addition, subtraction, division, or multiplication—you can use between the two numbers to get the highest result. Subtract that number from 100. Continue until you arrive at or below zero as quickly as possible.

Now play the game in a way that must get you exactly to zero. How is this a different problem? What do you know and what do you need to know? How can you reuse your thinking? Can you mentally test an operation before writing it on the paper? These are great ways of thinking like a computer programmer!

Glossary

access: The ability to use or enter something.

array: A group of numbers or symbols that are arranged in rows and columns.

define: To describe something clearly and completely.

efficient: Done in the quickest, best way possible.

implement: To carry out.

incorporate: To combine something with something else.

module: A part of a computer program that does a particular job.

obvious: Easy to see or notice.

prior: Earlier in time or order.

routine: A sequence of computer instructions for performing a particular task.

strategy: A plan of action to achieve a goal.

variable: A quantity that may change when other conditions change.

Index

Websites

Due to the changing nature of Internet links, PowerKids Press has developed an online list of websites related to the subject of this book. This site is updated regularly. Please use this link to access the list: www.powerkidslinks.com/kcc/prog